Original title:
Entangled in Ivy

Copyright © 2025 Creative Arts Management OÜ
All rights reserved.

Author: Julian Prescott
ISBN HARDBACK: 978-1-80567-330-9
ISBN PAPERBACK: 978-1-80567-629-4

## In the Grasp of Greenery

In a garden of giggles, I tripped on a vine,
It wrapped 'round my ankles, oh what a design!
The mailman was watching, he nearly fell too,
"Just a friendly plant!" I shouted, "How do you do?"

A bark from the bush, a laugh from a flower,
They plotted my stumble, they had all the power!
With leaves high-fiving, and petals that cheer,
My dance with the weeds has become quite the smear.

## Entwined with Life's Ivy

Oh, what a mess, I can't find my shoes,
They've run off with a shrub, it refuses to lose!
Raccoons are chuckling, they've joined in the fun,
As I dive in the thickets, I'm not yet done!

The garden's a party, with laughter and cheer,
Who knew that my sneakers would vanish so near?
A tumble, a roll, then a slip on a weed,
Dear plants, could you kindly let me proceed?

## The Silent Dance of Vines

The tendrils are twirling in a swirly waltz,
I'm caught in this tango, oh, what are the faults?
My hat's gone rogue, it's stuck on a leaf,
With nature's mischief, I'm dancing in grief!

The squirrels are laughing, their cheeks full of nuts,
While I'm stuck in a twist, oh life, aren't you nuts?
The daisies are smirking, with petals so bright,
Turning my folly into their funny plight.

## A Serpent's Caress

What's this creeping hug? It's around my waist!
With a squeeze from the flora, I'm feeling disgraced.
"Just a friend!" I holler, as it twirls with glee,
This cheeky green fellow seems fond of me!

The sun's in on it, with a wink and a grin,
My dance partner's bright and I can't help but spin.
A chuckle from branches, a chime from the breeze,
I'm caught in this merry green spiral with ease.

## The Lattice of Forgotten Dreams

In a garden where the weeds play,
The gnomes complain, 'It's our off-day!'
A snail slips by, oh what a race,
While daisies giggle, keeping pace.

The fence is choked with tales of old,
Of lovers lost and secrets told.
A hangout spot for bugs at night,
They gossip under the moonlight.

The sun peeks through a leafy veil,
A squirrel tells tales of his last fail.
He tried to leap, but missed the swing,
Now he's the joke of everything.

In this maze where laughter grows,
Even the thorns have punchlines, who knows?
With tangled roots like twisted fate,
Life's just a jest we all await.

## **Cloaked in Nature's Embrace**

In nature's hug where mischief blooms,
There's laughter echoing through the rooms.
A squirrel's hat made from a leaf,
He wears it proud, though it's brief.

The flowers sway, a jolly dance,
While bees attempt a clumsy prance.
An ant slips by, his load so grand,
He fumbles but takes it all in hand.

A frog croaks jokes that make us grin,
About a snail who dreamed of being thin.
The worms are laughing in their beds,
While spiders weave their tales with threads.

Beneath the arch of twisting vines,
Where nature's humor often shines,
Life's a punchline, quick and spry,
In this green haven, we all fly.

# A Tapestry of Twisting Leaves

A tapestry of greens and browns,
Where creatures roam in silly gowns.
A hedgehog sports a leafy hat,
While crickets chirp, 'What's up with that?'

The branches creak with a jolly tune,
As raccoons hold a wild afternoon.
They debate who's the best at hide and seek,
While the sun dips low, causing a squeak.

A butterfly lands, quite the flirt,
On a flower dressed in fancy dirt.
She flutters by, all charm and grace,
But trips on dew; what an awkward face!

In this wild world, fun's never far,
With friends like these, we raise the bar.
Leaves chuckle and trees sway in glee,
Join the laughter, it's the place to be.

## Secrets Beneath the Canopy

Secrets hide where shadows play,
Under the trees, come what may.
A raccoon moving with grace and flair,
Stole the picnic—what a bear!

The squirrels giggle, tails in a twist,
As ants plot a grand heist, can't be missed.
They form a line, their spirits high,
Hoping to snatch the last blueberry pie.

The whispers of leaves tell tales so bold,
Of acorns that dream of glittering gold.
Each tiny seed has a funny tale,
Of how they danced in the springtime gale.

So come and join this leafy jest,
Where nature always knows best.
Amid the giggles and laughter's glow,
Life's a comedy, that's how we grow.

## Woven Through the Canopy

A vine slipped on a shoe,
It laughed, 'Now I'm a shoe!'
Leaves danced in silly glee,
While squirrels held a tea party.

A bug thought it was a seat,
But found it way too sweet.
The branches did a jig,
As frogs croaked out a gig.

Twisting around each branch,
The sunlight caught the chance.
A riot of green and cheer,
The forest laughed, we could hear.

Underneath the leafy dome,
A snail navigates his home.
With a flip and flair, he's off,
While a rabbit just scoffs.

## The Secret Staccato of Growth

In the quiet, plants conspire,
With roots that never tire.
A shout from the lettuce bed,
"Oh, watch out for my head!"

Between the thyme and sage,
A snicker from the sage.
"Let's grow taller, it's time,"
As the basil starts to rhyme.

A dandelion sneezes loud,
In a corner, feeling proud.
Photosynthesis comes to play,
While the parsley sings away.

Little sprouts, so spry and bright,
Leap around with sheer delight.
A leaf's wink and a wink back,
Nature's own tango track.

## Dreams Wound Tight in Leaves

Underneath the leafy cloak,
A worm recites a joke.
"I wriggle just for fun,
But I'm still not done!"

Till the breeze took it away,
He danced without delay.
A flower blushed and sighed,
"Is he this spry or just fried?"

In the shade, a lazy bee,
Sipped nectar with glee.
"Guess who's buzzing this way?"
He slurred with a sunny sway.

Climbing up a twisted vine,
The critters wove a line.
With laughter, they couldn't believe,
The jester in every leaf.

## Bound by Botanical Threads

A fern wore a party hat,
"Time to dance!" said the cat.
With a wiggle of his tail,
He started a leafy trail.

"Watch the petals, don't slip!"
The daisies began to flip.
With a stomp and a shake,
They celebrated their break.

A tangle of roots did tease,
Chasing swarms of buzzing bees.
"Caught you!" they buzzed with pride,
As they danced from side to side.

In a world all wrapped around,
Life is where fun is found.
Among the greens and the browns,
Joy springs up from beneath the ground.

## The Climb Toward Unseen Light

With tendrils tickling my shoe,
I'm not sure what to do.
Old vines whisper secrets right,
As I stumble toward the light.

Each branch a jester in glee,
Laughing at clumsy me.
I leap but the leaves conspire,
To trap me in their leafy fire.

My hat gets snagged, oh dear me!
Is that a squirrel up a tree?
I trip over roots thick and slow,
Nature's slapstick show in tow.

Yet onward I laugh, what a sight,
This chase brings sheer delight.
With vines dancing like a ballet,
I'll reach the sun—someday, hooray!

## Roots of the Overgrown Heart

Tangled roots weave tales of yore,
In this rambling forest floor.
My heart grows heavy, then light as air,
With every step, it sheds a care.

Oh roots, they giggle as I prance,
Seizing every chance to dance.
I'll wear this crown of nature's jest,
Forget the trials, just have zest!

Amidst the weeds, my heart skips beats,
As laughter and clumsiness meets.
Beneath the echoes of playful trees,
I find joy in nature's tease.

With each turn, a twisty fate,
In this green giggle land, I await.
Though vines may pull my feet apart,
They'll never snare my sprightly heart!

## Echoes of Verdant Whispers

Listen close to leafy tales,
Where every shriek and giggle sails.
The trees sing low, the flowers beam,
Nature's funny little dream.

A prankster breeze rustles my hair,
As rodents plot with utmost care.
I trip and tumble, in the dell,
Over moss that seems to dwell.

These whispers continue to tease,
Imitating bees' sweet buzz of ease.
I grin at vines that know my plight,
Wrapping me up in pure delight.

But in this chaos, joy ignites,
Like sun beaming through wild nights.
In every tangle, humor hides,
Within the woods, where laughter abides!

## Nature's Veiled Intricacies

Through leafy veils, I make my way,
In this wild, whimsical ballet.
The flora laughs with every bend,
Inviting me to play and pretend.

A sneaky branch gives me a poke,
Am I a foolish, hapless joke?
But oh! How I dance with vines so grand,
A tangled game, hand in hand.

Mushrooms giggle in patches bright,
Chasing shadows, avoiding fright.
Nature's script is drawn with jest,
Pulling pranks, in jest, no rest.

With wire-like roots and curling ferns,
In every twist, the laughter churns.
Here, life is simply filled with play,
In intricate ways, we find our way!

## Intrigue Among Leaping Vines

In a garden full of tricks,
Vines play hide and seek,
They wrap around my ankles,
And giggle when I peek.

A squirrel runs by, quite bold,
With a stash of nuts to find,
But those vines grab him too,
And leave him in a bind.

Chasing shadows, racing leaves,
A dance that never stops,
I trip on roots like clumsy kids,
And everyone just hops.

With a twist and merry laugh,
These leafy pranks unfold,
While blossoms bloom with secrets,
Of stories yet untold.

## Lattice of Lost Affections

Within the latticework of green,
I send a note with glee,
To my crush beneath the leaves,
They trade it for a bee.

The flowers chuckle softly,
As my hope begins to sway,
For every love-filled message,
Another vine's in the way.

With tangled roots of friendship,
Entwined yet far apart,
I swear the garden's laughing,
At the folly of my heart.

Still, I toss my dreams like seeds,
In this quirky planting bed,
Some may sprout, some may not,
But laughter's always fed.

## Silent Hopscotch of the Climbing Heart

Jumping from stone to stone,
A hopscotch of pure cheer,
With vines that sway and giggle,
And tickle every ear.

The leaves start doing cartwheels,
As roses clap their hands,
In a game of silent laughter,
While ivy makes its plans.

I step on petals soft and shy,
They bloom with bright delight,
But each step leads to mischief,
In this bouncy, leafy flight.

With a wink, the garden whispers,
Join the hopscotch parade,
Where hearts and vines keep playing,
And joy will never fade.

## The Whimsy of Wandering Stems

Oh, the whiskers of the stems,
They tickle at my nose,
As I wander through the paths,
Where silly laughter grows.

A twisty vine pulls at my coat,
With a nudge that feels like fun,
I spin and twirl, I laugh aloud,
As the chasing has begun.

The green parade keeps giggling,
While sunbeams join the show,
And petals burst like confetti,
In this botanical throw.

So here's to stems that wander,
Their antics light and free,
In the realm of goofy greens,
Where every heart can see.

## The Embrace of Ancient Growth

In the forest, vines do sway,
They like to steal your breath away.
Climbing high, they make a fuss,
Wrapping 'round you like a bus!

You stroll with pride, it's all a game,
But suddenly it's not the same.
Your feet now tied, you do a jig,
A swift two-step is now quite big!

With each step, they pull you tight,
You're dancing with a leafy sprite.
A giggle slips, a chuckle bursts,
Who knew that plants could quench your thirst?

A tangled waltz with leafy friends,
This party clearly never ends.
With roots and fronds, you cha-cha-chase,
Together, in this green embrace!

## Nature's Rhapsody of Climbing Dreams

Vines weave tales both bold and bright,
Each step a challenge in the light.
Your shoes, once shiny, now are worn,
A climbing plant is slightly scorned!

Hitching rides on limbs and leaves,
A dance of nature that deceives.
You giggle as they drag you near,
What's that smell? Oh, dear, it's clear!

Their green attire has got some flair,
But watch your head! You've got to care.
With sticky hugs, they share a grin,
Says the sapling, "Let's swing again!"

Nature hums a silly tune,
Beneath the sun and silver moon.
With every leaf, you bend and sway,
You're just the punchline of their play!

## The Clutch of Wild Embrace

A vine pops up to say, "Hello!"
With leafy arms that start to grow.
You laugh, you spin, you take a leap,
But who knew nature's hugs run deep?

It wraps around your knees so tight,
You giggle, "What a funny sight!"
With serpentine grace, it takes a ride,
A green and jolly vine-y slide!

The jokes they tell, the laughs they cheer,
As you cling to the bark, much to your fear.
With every twist, you lose your way,
They say, "Stay still! We're here to play!"

From tree to tree, a frolic chase,
You tumble down in leafy lace.
Caught and caught, what a wild charade,
With friends, the vines' grand serenade!

## Fragments of Green Enchantment

In this jungle, chaos reigns,
A leafy crown adorns your brains.
What's that noise? A creeper shrieks,
With laughter loud, nature tweaks!

You walk with grace, you think you rock,
But soon you're wedged in nettle shock.
A leafy hug that's oh so snug,
Turns a stroll into a funky tug!

The squirrels giggle from above,
As you wrestle with your leafy glove.
A tap dance starts, its roots compose,
While vines play tricks on your old clothes!

Each sprawl and twist is pure delight,
You twirl with glee through day and night.
With green enchantment all around,
You're the star of this leafy ground!

## Labyrinth of Leafy Tangles


In a forest where vines conspire,
Snakes of green dance, never tire.
Hiding mice in leafy coats,
Wearing hats made out of oats.

A squirrel spins a silly tale,
About a mouse who stole a veil.
With branches whispering their joke,
The laughter yields a leafy smoke.

But the owl hoots with wise intent,
Beware the prank of nature's bent.
For every twist and turn you take,
A berry might just cause a quake.

Oh, the joy of wandering wide,
In a maze where fables abide.
With roots that giggle, branches tease,
In this tangle, we bend our knees.

### **Secrets in the Climbing Shadows**

Hidden secrets on the wall,
As ivy vines begin to crawl.
Ticklish tendrils, giggles shared,
In the dark, surprises bared.

A caterpillar throws a bash,
With a party that's quite the splash.
The beetles boogie, having fun,
Until the moon is finally done.

Green tendrils hide the cheeky snare,
As shadows prance without a care.
Whispers echo through the drape,
Tales of nature's silly shape.

In this ballet of leafy cheer,
Even worms can find their beer.
The garden sings a joyful tune,
Where every plant's a merry boom.

# Twine of Nature's Grip

Ribbons twist and turns around,
With roots that jive upon the ground.
A dandelion bows its head,
While tulips laugh beneath their bed.

Spiders weave their crafty lace,
Inviting all, their games we chase.
Fluffy clouds peek through the green,
While critters dance to nature's scene.

Bumblebees wear hats of fluff,
Buzzing through their silly stuff.
With every swat, the dance goes wild,
Reminding us that life's a child.

So tiptoe through this playful zone,
Where laughter reigns and whimsy's grown.
In nature's grip, we swing and dip,
Within this twine, we lose our grip.

## **Veils of Verdant Desire**

Behind the leaves, a secret sigh,
Nature wears a bright bow tie.
With tendrils draped in funny style,
Even the trees can't help but smile.

A lizard poses for a pic,
While crickets play a little trick.
With every rustle, gossip spreads,
The garden's tales dance in our heads.

In shadows soft, the jokes might blend,
Where sunshine meets each playful trend.
Mossy cushions, where we sup,
Even frogs can't help but jump up.

So roam through vines and grassy beds,
Where whispers tickle little heads.
In veils of green with puns implied,
We find our joy, our hearts open wide.

## The Lattice of Lustrous Life

In a garden where the green vines play,
A squirrel's got a dance, what a display!
He twirls and leaps, quite the spry chap,
While holders of the lettuce shout, "Stop that rap!"

A snail with dreams of racing fast,
Pondering how his shell's been cast.
He smiles and thinks, 'I'll win this game!'
Unaware the turtle's already on the flame!

The plants all giggle as they sway,
While flowers gossip about the day.
Who knew a vine could twist with glee?
Oh, the secrets of green jubilee!

And in this patch of leafy delight,
Even the weeds think they're polite.
Together they form quite the riot,
In this lush world, everyone's a quiet diet!

## Enveloping Nature's Threads

A spider spun her web with flair,
While ants all wondered if they dare.
"Can we walk that line without a fall?"
"Sure, just avoid the sticky squall!"

The daisies hatched a plan so sly,
With colors bright, they aimed to fly.
"Let's dress up in the sun's warm rays,
And prank the bees in every way!"

A cactus craved a wild night out,
He donned his ferns without a doubt.
With spiky charm and a wig of green,
He wore a crown, oh so serene!

In this tangled patch of vibrant fun,
Nature laughs, for no one has to run.
With roots and leaves in raucous pleasure,
This botanical life, a treasure beyond measure!

## The Intricate Weave of Botanics

In the forest, vines have quite the plight,
Attempting to dance under moonlight.
A raccoon chuckles, on a branch up high,
"Who knew trying to tango could make you cry?"

Moss decided to throw a little bash,
While ferns and blooms joined in with panache.
"Let's twist and shout till dawn breaks through!"
Said a dandelion with a swirl of dew.

Grapes overhead plotted a caper,
While lettuce leaves dressed as a draper.
In this green carnival, all joined in,
Nature's laughter, a resounding din!

Each leaf and stem, a tale to be told,
In whimsical tones, both brash and bold.
So here's to the green, with its glorious mess,
In this hallowed grove, let's all confess!

## Growth's Tender Thralldom

A fern claimed the title of the gossip queen,
Spouting tales of things she'd seen.
"Oh, the sunflowers think they're so grand,
But wait 'til they see today's band!"

The rocks rolled their eyes at clumsy plants,
"I see your wobbles, do the ants?"
They chuckled and cackled, so loud and proud,
As petals fluttered, forming a crowd.

The moon eavesdropped on their silly cheers,
Whispers of moss brought laughter and jeers.
"Oh, my dear blooms, so tender and sweet,
Life's just a frolic, on this leafy street!"

As roots danced deep in soft earthen beds,
Flora shared stories, as laughter spreads.
In this home where green antics thrive,
Nature's leaps invite us to be alive!

## Lush Embraces and Hidden Paths

Among the green, there's quite a mix,
A leaf that laughs, it gives me kicks.
I trip and tumble, what a sight,
A vine gives chase, I'm in for a fright!

With every twist, I find my way,
Through leafy mazes, come what may.
A friendly shrub, it makes a tease,
I swear it giggles just like bees!

A squirrel scurries, steals my hat,
It leaps through branches, just like that.
I yell, "Hey buddy, you forgot!"
But ivy whispers, "This is your lot!"

In playful loops, I'm lost, it seems,
Among the flora, I chase my dreams.
Oh, tangled fun in leafy zones,
Nature's tricks, no need for phones!

## Confinement of Flourishing Shadows

In shadows deep, I dance around,
With vines and leaves, I'm tightly bound.
I wave to flowers that giggle so,
While roots below decide where I go!

A creeping thing, it gives me hugs,
While I do pirouettes, what a plug!
"Oh dear," I shout, "I need a tea!"
But fronds just chuckle, "Stay here with me!"

A knotty twist, a leafy dance,
Each step I take, I risk romance.
I quicken pace, but ivy pulls tight,
I scream, "This plant loves me too much, right?"

In nature's grip, hilarity blooms,
As every shrub becomes my room.
I smile wide, it's quite a spree,
In this green cage, I'm wild and free!

## Nature's Binding Serenade

Oh, sweet serenade of tangled glee,
I'm stuck with plants and a buzzing bee.
A leafy chorus sings my name,
While roots wrap tight, it's all the same!

I dance with stems, a duet grand,
Petals laugh, they understand.
In this green jail, I spin and twirl,
With laughter echoing all around the whirl.

A lizard nods, it winks with glee,
It states, "My friend, this is the key!"
To frolic here in nature's jest,
Where every leaf knows how to rest.

A serenade of rustling sound,
While vines and flowers wrap me round.
In this embrace, I cheerfully sing,
Oh nature's jest, what joy you bring!

## The Thicket's Tender Touch

In thickets dense, I hear the call,
A pushy vine that's quite enthralled.
"Come join the fun!" it seems to shout,
While giggling blooms dance all about!

I leap and hop, with branches near,
But true delight becomes my fear.
With every grab, they tease and play,
"Will you escape? Or here you'll stay!"

A rabbit chips in on my side,
"Don't be so tense, just enjoy the ride!"
He scampers off, the thicket sighs,
"More fun with friends and a few surprise!"

I yield to laughter, no longer shy,
In tangled threads, I learn to fly.
In this green hug, joy takes the lead,
With every giggle, I plant a seed!

## Patterns woven in Green

I found a frog in my shoe,
He said, "These vines make quite a zoo!"
With every step, he would croak,
I laughed so hard, I nearly choked.

The garden's a maze, leafy and loud,
It's hard to find my way, I'm proud!
The plants hug tightly, it's quite a scene,
Next up is dinner—hop on the green machine!

A squirrel popped by, with a nut in tow,
He wiggled and danced, put on a show.
The flowers giggled, swayed to the beat,
In this leafy world, life feels like a treat.

With nature's craziness, I can't complain,
Each twist and turn brings joy, not pain.
So here's to gardens, wild and bright,
Where every petal's a reason for delight.

## The Green Tangle's Song

Amidst the leaves, I hear a tune,
A caterpillar dances, under the moon.
He sways to rhythms that only he knows,
While a snail gives a shout, in quick little throes.

The vines all giggle, tickling the air,
As they weave a melody, happy and rare.
Each branch a partner, twirling in glee,
While I sit and laugh at this green jamboree.

A bird swings by with a chirpy request,
"Join us, dear friend, it's quite a fest!"
With laughter and hops, I leap in delight,
The tangled green dance lasts all through the night.

So here's to the chaos of nature's big show,
With funny little critters putting on a toe-to-toe.
Let the vine-kissed giggles flow free as the song,
In this wild and nutty green wonderland, we belong.

## Shadows Under the Climbing Canopy

Under the leaves, a secret lie,
A tortoise and rabbit whisper and sigh.
"Hey, slowpoke! Let's race, no peeking allowed!"
The shadows laugh softly, forming a crowd.

The breeze tickles grass, like a playful tease,
While a squirrel plots mischief with acorn ease.
A shadow collides with a jumpy young fox,
They hide from the world, behind knotted locks.

As the sun sets low, it paints us gold,
While fungi giggle at stories untold.
The green canopy sways, the sky is our stage,
In this quirky dance, we're all the same age.

So let's celebrate life, with all that it brings,
In laughter and antics, like shadows, we cling.
The night is our friend, with whispers so glum,
Under the climbing canopy, we play till we're numb.

## Love Knotted with Leaves


In a patch of green, two hearts made a vow,
With ivy's embrace, they felt love somehow.
A twist here, a turn, they romanced the plants,
Even roses blushed, doing a waltz dance.

They spun through the flora, giggling with glee,
"I'm rooted in you!" said the big oak tree.
With laughter that rustled through garden and glade,
Their love grew wild, not a single charade.

As sunlight dappled, they whispered through ferns,
Each knot and each loop brought delightful turns.
The daisies applauded, swaying to the beat,
While bees buzzed sweet, delivering love's treat.

So raise a glass, let's toast to the green,
Where love and laughter spin every scene.
In this foliage romance, forever it weaves,
A humorous tale, where joy never leaves.

# The Symphony of the Climbing Green

A vine tickles the garden chair,
While I nap without a care.
It weaves a tune both loud and shy,
As squirrels dance and butterflies fly.

A trumpet plant starts to play,
With flowers that giggle through the day.
The creeping green can't help but tease,
A rhapsody of rustling leaves.

The grass joins in, a chorus bright,
While critters cavort, oh what a sight!
A thistle hums a prickly strum,
While nature's jesters loudly drum.

Oh, symphony of twists and bends,
A concert where the fun never ends!
With laughter caught in every vine,
In this eccentric garden shrine.

## Essays of the Overgrown Path

Stumbling upon a leafy tome,
Words sprout where no one roams.
A hedgehog pens its dubious plight,
On a leaf at the edge of night.

The stones are editors, standing tall,
Critiquing every slip and fall.
A worm is typing, oh so slow,
With beetles as the audience row.

The path is long, but fun awaits,
In snickers sung by garden mates.
While shadows vie for space to play,
Giggles echo, come what may.

In this odd classroom of the wild,
Nature teaches with glee, so mild.
Essays written, laughter shared,
In every word, kindness declared.

## Shadows Merging with the Fern

Whispers of shadows in leafy dress,
Twirl and dive into a playful mess.
The fern giggles, waving its fans,
As sunlight paints a world of plans.

A shadow slips without a care,
Tripping lightly on the air.
It winks at flowers stacked like pies,
While bees buzz by with friendly sighs.

The ferns, they giggle, swaying wide,
As creatures hide then jump outside.
A dance of stealth, a game anew,
Where shadows play and ferns pursue.

Mirthful laughter in dizzying rounds,
Where silliness and joy abounds.
In this realm of whimsical turn,
Shadows laugh, and the ferns will churn.

## The Tangle's Timid Secret

In a tangle, secrets intertwine,
Laughter hidden, like a fine wine.
A sprout shyly whispers of a dream,
In a world where nothing's as it seems.

The curl of a vine, a curious twist,
Winks at critters who can't resist.
A frog with a crown sings offbeat tunes,
To lull the stars that hug the moon.

The timid secret gives a smirk,
As squirrels plot some mischief at work.
With every tug and playful yelp,
The tangle giggles, just like help.

From gnomes to trolls, tales unfold,
In a world where laughs are pure gold.
Whispers of joy in every nook,
This tangled patch is worth a look!

## **Threads of Green Confessions**

In the garden, things go wild,
A gnome winks, very beguiled.
Vines twist like a playful cat,
Who knew plants could act like that?

My hat's caught in a tangle spree,
A clump of leaves laughing at me.
The snails race with a clumsy glee,
Oh, what a leafy jubilee!

Rabbits giggle, leaping around,
In this forest, whimsy is found.
But oh, the sun's a blinding tease,
With every step, my shoes get squeezed.

Under the green, secrets unfold,
Where whispers dance, and tales are told.
A lizard grins, one eye on my shoe,
In this tangled mess, I'm quite the zoo!

## The Clutch of the Whispering Thicket

In shadows deep where critters play,
The branches shimmer, sway and sway.
I stumbled, tripped, landed with a thud,
Surrounded by a swirling flood.

The bushes snicker, leaves a-chatter,
As I wrestle with a snoozing batter.
A squirrel clapped, oh what a show,
I swear these greens are in on the joke!

Thorns poke at my polka-dot attire,
Yet laughter sings, it's not dire.
A frog croaks his chart-topping note,
While I ponder why my dignity floats.

Every twig holds a secret chat,
Of dandelions and a chunky rat.
A butterfly guffaws, fluttering fast,
In this verdant chaos, hilarity lasts!

## Labored Locks of the Growing Green

My hair's a wild jungle, it's true,
A nest of leaves, what a view!
Brushing it out takes an hour or two,
The birds think it's home, how about you?

Each morning I wrestle, tug and pull,
My brush gets stuck, it's quite a duel.
"Must be a grapevine," I quip with a grin,
But the ladybug cheers, "Let the fun begin!"

In the chaos of curls and sprout,
Oh, what an uproar, I can't live without!
Bees buzz by, thinking they'd thrive,
A beauty trend gone wrong, I barely survive.

When friends arrive for a laugh and a tease,
They can't help but giggle at the leafy freeze.
With every snatch, a legendary embrace,
In my tangled mane, I've found my place!

## Lurking in the Leafy Shadows

Beneath the boughs where whispers creep,
I find myself in a leafy heap.
A raccoon nods, wearing a hat,
Am I a guest or a welcome mat?

Some say it's magic, the vines that sway,
I swear they giggle at my ballet.
With every turn, I bump and lurch,
In this green embrace, I lose my search.

A 'whoosh' from bushes, a giggle nearby,
It's like being chased by a friendly pie!
Roots sticking out, they plan my defeat,
In this leafy realm, life can't be beat!

But as I dance, stumble and spin,
The trees applaud my clumsy twin.
Oh, laughter blooms where the wild things grow,
Who knew the thicket had such a show?

## **Curling Earthbound Wishes**

In a garden, weeds plot and play,
Twisting my shoelaces in disarray.
Laughter erupts with every trip,
As they dance around, a sneaky grip.

Wishes float low in the humid air,
Getting snagged on branches without a care.
Dreams of heights, but oh, what a plight,
These vines are giggling, pulling me tight.

Their playful embrace, so snug and round,
While I hop and stumble on the ground.
With vines like these, it's hard to strut,
But they keep my feet stuck, oh, what a rut!

So I'll shout my dreams to the leafy crew,
Hoping they hear—yes, you know what to do!
With a flick and a twist, let me be free,
And leave my shoes in the mess of glee!

## Veins of the Wild

In the thicket, all things abound,
With jellybeans stuck to the ground.
A critter pops up, wins the snack,
A merry chase—I'll take it back!

But the vines are laughing, what a jest,
Hiding my jellybeans, they're the best!
A tapestry woven with quirky flair,
I chase my treats through the leafy lair.

Nature's jesters, they pull and stretch,
Playing pranks on friends—I'm quite the fetch!
With vines of green that entice and tease,
Who needs a game when it's so easy to squeeze?

Oh, vines, you tricksters, with your leafy charms,
Making mischief with your sassy arms.
I'll be the jester of this carnival spree,
If only these vines didn't make a fool out of me!

## The Green Shroud's Lure

Underneath the leafy spread,
A dragonfly gleefully fled.
But wait! What's this? A leafy snare,
Whirled around, I'm caught unaware!

The green shroud giggles with playful cheer,
As I tumble headfirst, no hope to steer.
Flailing about, a wild goose chase,
Aerial acrobatics in this plant-based race!

With laughs from below, I give a shout,
"Release me now!" as I spin about.
Just when I thought the game was set,
The vines knew better—no chance to get wet!

Stuck in green with a smile so wide,
With leafy hugs, how can one chide?
In nature's embrace, it's quite the ruse,
While I giggle in vines—oh, what a muse!

## In the Depths of Leafy Darkness

In shadows deep, where mischief brews,
The foliage whispers and giggles ensues.
Beneath the gloom where twigs align,
A party of critters sips sweet brine.

Lighting up dreams with bright, shiny eyes,
Raccoons in tuxedos, what a surprise!
They swipe my popcorn without a care,
As the vines chuckle, all aware!

This leafy den, a hub of delight,
Where shadows thrum with laughter at night.
With every rustle, my heart skips a beat,
Who knew humor thrived in this verdant seat?

So here I sit, chuckling away,
Caught in the laughter, come what may.
In this leafy party, I found my place,
With vines and critters in a merry chase!

## **The Enigma of Nature's Embrace**

In a garden wild and free,
A frog sings off-key,
A squirrel steals my sandwich,
While vines weave quite mischievously.

The flowers giggle in the breeze,
While ants dance with such ease,
A bee bumps into my nose,
Nature plays tricks, if you please.

A rabbit hops with flair and style,
Wearing leaves like a natural dial,
As I trip over roots and stones,
Outdoor adventures make me smile.

The trees whisper secrets so sly,
Encouraging me to give it a try,
But tangled up in greens so bright,
I wonder if I'll ever fly.

## **Tendrils of Forgotten Tales.**

In the forest where oddthings roam,
I found a lizard with a tiny comb,
He styled his spikes for the evening show,
While the flowers laughed, 'He's lost at home!'

A vine that dared to take a leap,
Wrapped around my legs, oh, what a creep!
I thought I'd found a friend so true,
But now I'm struggling, and can't make a peep.

Snails in hats, creeping with grace,
Trying to win the slowest race,
I cheer them on, feeling quite spry,
Just pray they don't pick up the pace!

Even the mushrooms, small and round,
Are telling tales that astound,
Who knew fungi were such good friends?
In this venue of strange, I'm bound!

## Whispers of the Green Embrace

Little vines prance, a curious sight,
Tickling my ankles, full of delight,
I laugh as they pull, a comical dance,
    Nature's jesters in morning light.

A caterpillar's wearing a tie,
Dreaming of wings, oh me, oh my,
With a wink and a wiggle, he says, 'Just you wait!'
    In this leafy circus, how time does fly!

The trees gossip like old friends do,
Sharing stories of what we pursue,
While dandelions burst forth with cheer,
    Pretending they're actors in a green-view.

Bumblebees sipping from petals so sweet,
Join in the fun with their buzzing beat,
Here in this world where laughter's the key,
    I'll stay forever, avoiding defeat.

## Snare of the Silent Vines

In a patch of green where shadows play,
Vines conspire to have their way,
I wander, laughing, quite unaware,
They trip me up at the close of the day.

A hedgehog rolls by, oh what a scene,
Decked in flowers, looking quite keen,
He chuckles at me as I tumble down,
In this green realm, I feel like a queen!

Mossy rocks hide secrets untold,
With stories of days from the ages old,
But every time I lean down to see,
I'm snagged by a vine—oh, bold!

Yet here I find joy, silliness reigns,
In this tangled mess where humor sustains,
Nature's jokes can't be outdone,
As I scamper through the refrains!

## Entwined Fates Beneath the Arbor

In the garden where we play,
Laughter drapes like vines on display,
A leaf fell down, it hit my head,
Now I'm convinced it's wisdom spread.

The squirrels dance, a cheeky show,
Stealing acorns, on the go,
I trip on roots, they chitter loud,
Growing wiser, or lost in the crowd.

Colors bloom in silly hues,
Petals giggle with morning dew,
We mold our dreams, like ivy's reach,
Nature's humor, a leafy speech.

So raise a glass, let's toast the cheer,
To tangled fates that keep us near,
Underneath this leafy dome,
We find a way to call it home.

## The Cloistered Path of Growth


A pathway lined with sneaky greens,
Whispering secrets, bursting seams,
I walked too close and lost my shoe,
Now ivy claims me—who knew?

With every twist, I grunt and slide,
Nature's joke, a bumpy ride,
A rabbit giggles, hops right past,
While I'm held tight, the vine's steadfast.

In this maze, I can't see clear,
Yet every turn ignites a cheer,
A friend of mine, he brings a snack,
But ivy stole it—who's got my back?

So here I laugh, embraced by green,
In nature's clutches, we are seen,
Time to unwind, let craziness flow,
In this cloistered maze, I'm never low.

## **Ivy-Flecked Reflections**

A mirror shows my leafy flair,
With tendrils creeping, taking care,
I wave to weeds, they wave right back,
We share coffee on this leafy rack.

Bright blooms wink, they know the game,
Of growing wild, with no shame,
I lost my glasses, they're in the patch,
Foliage laughs, I make a match.

Clovers tease as I trip and roll,
With unsteady grace, I find my soul,
In this green wonderland, I play,
A comedic dance, come what may.

So take a glance, don't take it hard,
In ivy's arms, we find our yard,
With every laugh, each silly jest,
Reflections stay, and we're all blessed.

## Melodies from the Green Abyss

In the thicket, a tune takes flight,
Leaves rustle softly, a playful sight,
A pair of frogs sing off-key loud,
Echoing laughter, they're quite proud.

Roots make my shoes their favorite toy,
Oh! What a clumsy tale to enjoy,
With every skip, I find delight,
Dancing through shadows, pure and light.

The branches sway to a rhythm divine,
Tangled in humor, they intertwine,
A woodpecker joins for the grand finale,
While I'm caught giggling in this leafy gully.

So heed the call of this verdant cheer,
Let laughter out, set aside the fear,
For in this green abyss, I must confess,
Every note sings of nature's jest.

## The Snarl of Green Sentences

In the garden, plants conspire,
Climbing higher, they never tire.
Whispers of vines twist and twirl,
Telling tales of the leafy swirl.

A bushy beard on the old oak,
Jokes are traded, laughter's the poke.
A dandelion's fluff takes flight,
Landing where the sun shines bright.

The ivy grins with a cheeky wink,
As raccoons plot their next big prank.
Squirrels race in a nutty chase,
While turtles put on a sluggish face.

All onlookers in their green sport,
Join the fun in nature's court.
With every twist, a giggle ensues,
This leafy life sure knows how to amuse.

## Nature's Coiling Caress

Vines weave stories in summer's glow,
Caressing branches, putting on a show.
Laughter echoes where roots entwine,
Nature's tricks are simply divine.

A snail slips by, with great disdain,
While worms gossip in the soft rain.
Frogs croak rhythms of a merry song,
In this dance, nothing feels wrong.

Bumbling bees buzz with great zest,
Pollinating flowers, they never rest.
Amidst the chaos, a joyous spree,
Life's entanglements, wild and free.

With nature's touch, all woes unwind,
Vines tickling souls, joy intertwined.
Each leafy hug a quirky embrace,
In this woodland, we find our place.

## Embraces Wrought in Nature's Web

Webs of mischief in shades of green,
Bumblebees buzzing, a comical scene.
Laughter erupts as squirrels collide,
Chasing their tails with nothing to hide.

Sunlight dapples the clover patch,
Where ladybugs play and crickets hatch.
The tangled roots serve as the floor,
Of a dance party nature has in store.

With petals that giggle, the flowers sway,
A ruckus of colors brightening the day.
Thistles roll over, sharing a snort,
In a wild, leafy, uproarious sport.

Nature's comedy, sweetly absurd,
Vines and blooms, joined in a word.
Each twist and turn is a comic cue,
As laughter unfurls in the morning dew.

## The Soft Snare of the Wilderness


In the woods, vines make their claims,
Wrapping trees in their leafy games.
With a sly wink, they pull you close,
Nature's embrace, we love the most.

Frolicsome ferns flutter and prance,
While critters join in the wild dance.
Barking beetles host a show,
Under the canopy, where giggles flow.

The sun peeks through with a cheeky grin,
As tangled roots create a din.
Rabbits hop, trying to be sly,
While pigeons plot and dream to fly.

In this soft snare, we lose our way,
Charmed by nature's funny play.
With every rustle, a laugh we find,
In the forest's reach, we leave woes behind.

## The Enigma of the Ivy Cloak

A leafy cloak, so snug and tight,
I thought it was a fashion delight.
But here I am, held in its grip,
Like an awkward dance, a clumsy trip.

The neighbors stare, they point and laugh,
As I wiggle and squirm, what a gaffe!
"Look at that gardener, bound so neat,"
They giggle while I try to retreat.

The vines decide to make me their throne,
With every twist, I feel so alone.
A trendsetter I thought I would be,
Now I'm a spectacle—oh, joy for free!

But who knew plants had a sense of style?
They throw me a party, it's all worthwhile!
With laughter in leaves and joy in the air,
I guess being tangled has its own flair.

## Embrace of the Roving Roots

Roots that roam like mischievous elves,
Decided to tease, not leave me in delves.
They wrapped around me while I gardened,
Now I'm stuck with this nature as warden.

"Is this a vine or a snake?" I shout,
As I hop around, stuck in a clout.
With every twist, my fashion's gone wild,
I'm the laughingstock of this leafy child.

The bushes giggle, the flowers chime,
Each petal whispers, 'It's just a good time!'
So I dance with roots, with style unplanned,
In this botanical mess, I take a stand.

Who knew a stroll could result in such muck?
A hop, a skip, and then—what luck!
With laughter and laughter, I lose all woe,
These silly roots put on quite a show!

## The Binding of Botanicals

A garden rogue with mischief at play,
Thought I'd prune, not make a bouquet.
But the flora conspired, my limbs they did tame,
Now I'm stuck in this botanical game.

With vines for laces and leaves for charm,
I'm the latest fashion—albeit with harm.
"Who wore it best?" they'll say with a grin,
As I smile awkwardly, my struggle set in.

Every branch a joke, each petal a pun,
Who knew that gardening could be so fun?
I twitch, I laugh, all night I will stay,
Creating wild stories in a leafy ballet.

So let's raise a toast to this folly of green,
I'm 'in' with the plants, I'm their leafy queen!
In this tangled mess, I've found my delight,
As the garden chuckles at my botanic plight.

## Flourish and Fetters

In a world of flowers, I sought to shine,
But got stuck in a climber's design.
Now my friends come by with jokes and glee,
As I flail about like a leaf on a spree.

"Look at my outfit!" I boast with flair,
But the vines just grin, they don't seem to care.
Like a circus act, I've lost all my grace,
But who cares when you're wearing a green embrace?

A hop and a shake, they tighten their hold,
As I twirl around, feeling foolish, yet bold.
Each tendril a handshake, it hugs me so tight,
Can't tell if it's love or a leafy fright.

But give me my blooms and I'll grin through my fate,
In this wild party, I just celebrate!
With laughter and roots, in my leafy attire,
I'm the queen of the garden, my spirit's on fire!

## Whispers of Woven Green

In the garden, a plant took a leap,
Wrapped itself tight, made a cozy heap.
Said the flower to the bush with a grin,
"Did you see that? They're at it again!"

The sun came out, and the leaves had a chat,
"I'm stuck in this tangle, how about that?"
Laughter echoed where the twigs did weave,
A green comedy show, I wouldn't believe!

Vines on a fence were plotting a prank,
"Let's tie up the neighbor's cat by the flank!"
But the cat just yawned, and said, "Oh dear,
Not again! This is getting too clear!"

So beware of the green with a giggle and dance,
For they'll wrap you up in a leafy romance.
In the midst of their snickers and spirals so grand,
You'll find yourself joining their vine-laden band.

## Tangled Roots of Memory

In a forest thick, where the shrubberies grow,
Memories wriggle, like a wiggly show.
"Did you remember that time with the shroom?"
"Oh yes! We got lost in the plant's cozy room!"

Roots above ground, they tickled your toes,
"Don't mind me, I'm just here for the show!"
A squirrel chimed in, with a tail made of fluff,
"Do you think these vines have had quite enough?"

Laughter echoed where the daily grass met,
As the daisies whispered, "A brand new duet!"
Snaking and twisting, they danced through the night,
With a chorus of colors that felt just right.

In this quagmire of giggles and leafy delights,
Your heart finds a beat in the unraveling sights.
Each root tells a tale, each leaf sings a tune,
In the tangled embrace of a botanical cartoon!

## Embrace of the Climbing Veil

A vine hitched a ride on a fencepost so bold,
Whispered sweet secrets, a tapestry told.
"Life's a climb, don't you fret or frown!"
The daisies agreed, as they bobbed up and down.

Leaves tickled petals, made everyone giggle,
As they swayed in the breeze, doing a little wiggle.
A caterpillar laughed, said, "Join in the fun!"
"Why not? We'll party 'til the day is done!"

With a swish and a sway, they danced in a trance,
In the embrace of the green, they all took a chance.
"Let's poke a nosy neighbor while we're at it!"
And they plotted their scheme with a mischievous habit.

So if you wander where the tangles play sweet,
Watch for the vines and their joyful heartbeat.
They'll take you along on a whimsical ride,
In a leafy embrace where the laughter won't hide.

## **Shadows Among the Vines**

Among the shadows where the green leaves have met,
Lurk funny little critters, you won't soon forget.
A lizard slipped by with a waggle and wink,
"Watch your step; it's a slippery brink!"

In the twilight, the vines start to swing,
As the crickets serenade, they'll jitterbug and sing.
"What's that over there? Is it a bug or a shoe?"
"It's just Timmy, he's lost in the dew!"

With laughter among shadows, they created a scene,
Like a tangled-up circus, all sprightly and green.
"Join us, come hither, don't be shy or aloof!"
"But is it true that the vines tell the truth?"

As laughter erupted and the night wore thin,
They tangled together in a jovial spin.
So if you wander through the greenery game,
Remember the vine and their uproarious claim!

## Embrace of the Nature's Spire

In the garden, a vine went rogue,
Wrapping 'round my leg like a dog.
I tried to run, but she held tight,
Laughing softly, oh what a sight!

She sprouted leaves and took a stand,
Claiming my shoe as her piece of land.
"Just a moment!" I tried to plea,
"Must you be my new accessory?"

## The Tangle of Timeless Growth

There once was a bush that wanted a friend,
But its hugs, you see, would never end.
It wrapped my ankles in leafy lace,
Stumbling backward, I fell on my face!

It promised me joy in verdant cheer,
But all I got was dirt and a tear.
"Do you always have to be so clingy?"
Exclaimed I in jest, feeling quite stingy.

## Climbing Heart's Conundrum

A plant thought I had room to share,
Creeping up my back, without a care.
I giggled and squirmed, what a cute thrill,
But it just grinned, plotting my spill!

Each step I took, it grew more bold,
Just like a tale that never gets old.
"What's next, dear friend?" I asked with glee,
"A dance-off? A climb? Or just a spree?"

## **Greenery's Gentle Hold**

In the park, a vine did tease,
Winding 'round my knees with ease.
"Stand still!" it whispered, what a prank!
"Oh no, I've become a nature flank!"

With leafy fingers so sweet and sly,
It made a crown, oh my, oh my!
"Fancy a queen?" it swayed with grace,
But my rule was done—who needs that space?

## **The Rooted Affection**

In gardens lush where laughter grows,
The vines play tag with garden hose.
They tickle toes of passersby,
And whisper jokes, oh my, oh my!

With every twist and leafy prance,
They spin a tale, a leafy dance.
They tease the sun, they chase the breeze,
And hide from birds, oh what a tease!

Around the bench they curl and twist,
As if to say, you can't resist.
They hug the fence like best of friends,
Their leafy laughter never ends.

Though roots may cling in soil so deep,
These verdant jokers never sleep.
For in their world of shade and light,
Each day is filled with pure delight.

## **Serenity in the Sylvan Snare**

In tangled trails where giggles hide,
The leaves conspire, they're side by side.
A squirrel rides on creeping vine,
While I just watch and sip my wine!

The branches sway in playful cheer,
As if to say, come join us here!
A friendly sprout flicks dirt my way,
With every laugh, it begs to stay.

I trip on roots, but who's to blame?
These playful vines are not the same.
They pull me close, in jest, no fear,
With every fall, I cheer and leer!

Amongst the leaves, my heart takes flight,
In nature's grasp, all feels just right.
With laughter woven in the green,
I find true peace where joy's unseen.

## Wild Whispers in the Green Maze

Among the ferns, the secrets play,
A rustle here, a giggle there,
The ivy churns, it seems to say,
"Join in the fun, if you dare!"

Curly vines embrace the trees,
A game of hide-and-seek with bees.
The sun peeks through, a little tease,
While branches sway with playful ease.

The garden gnomes look quite bemused,
As ivy pulls them in, so used.
They grin and hug their leafy friends,
For camaraderie knows no ends!

In nature's play, we lose our way,
Yet find the joy that's here to stay.
With every twist, a giggle shared,
In green mazes, laughter's bared.

## The Ties that Vine

Oh, how they twist, those playful vines,
In knots and loops, like silly signs.
They pull you in, a gentle bind,
And laugh aloud, oh what a find!

A wallflower blushes, shy but bold,
As ivy's whispers take their hold.
In tiny fronds, such mischief brews,
Creating chaos, playful hues.

A picnic blanket's now a trap,
As tendrils wrap, like soft, green sap.
The sandwiches are not alone,
As vines declare, "This space is our throne!"

With every twist, a new surprise,
The garden's humor never dies.
So join the games, don't be shy,
For laughter's found where greens comply!

# Convergence of Nature's Heart

In a garden bustling with glee,
A worm wore glasses to see,
He bumped into a curious bee,
Who danced like he was wild and free.

The petals giggled, the leaves would sway,
As critters joined the vibrant ballet,
A snail remarked, "What a fine day!"
While ants strutted in their own parade.

With laughter echoing through the trees,
A frog croaked jokes, put minds at ease,
Nature's heart in joyful tease,
Embraced by moments such as these.

So if you stop, and take a glance,
You might just catch the vines' own dance,
Where every silly twist and chance,
Will make you smile and laugh, perchance.

## Ivy's Silent Serenade

In the garden where ivy plays,
It whispers secrets on sunny days,
A squirrel listens, his head in a haze,
As shadows twirl in humorous ways.

A cat with dreams of fine cuisine,
Stalks the ivy, looking quite keen,
But finds a rabbit, oh so mean,
Who taunts and darts with flair unseen.

The ivy giggles with vines entwined,
While buttercups sway, feeling so fine,
A dance of nature, silly and blind,
Creating laughter in every line.

So join the frolic beneath the green,
Where laughter's the thread, a joyful glean,
In this whimsical world, serene,
The ivy sings in a charming scene.

## The Lure of the Wandering Blades

A grass blade fancied a playful fling,
With a dandelion puff, she'd try to swing,
"Catch me if you can!" she'd giggle and sing,
As the breeze giggled, sending a spring.

A curious snail thought it a race,
With flopping cheeks, he tried to chase,
But fell on his shell, what a colorful face!
The laughter echoed, filling the space.

The blades all chuckled, swaying about,
While ladybugs joined the merry route,
A caterpillar spun tales, no doubt,
As nature danced, there arose a shout!

So in the garden where whimsy thrives,
Life's a jest, and fun derives,
Among the wandering blades, it survives,
Creating a laughter that always strives.

## Rooted Revelations Among the Vines

Beneath the vines, a secret's kept,
Where ants in tuxedos have merrily crept,
To a grand ol' party, no one except
The bugs and blooms are ready, prepped.

A flower tipped his petals high,
And said, "Let's toast to the butterfly!"
While laughing crickets crooned nearby,
As beetles danced, oh my, oh my!

The ivy swayed, pulled by the breeze,
Whispering tales of lovely trees,
Where roots entwined like old friends, please,
Shared hearty laughs and sneezed with ease.

So come, magnolia, join in this shindig,
Where laughter thrives and life's a big gig,
Among the vines, where joy's the jig,
Rooted in mirth, let's dance a fig!

www.ingramcontent.com/pod-product-compliance
Lightning Source LLC
Chambersburg PA
CBHW071827160426
43209CB00003B/230